When

Love,

Neva

Love!

Neva

When Pigs Fly

The Parent's Guide to Inspire Your Young Entrepreneur

Neva Lee Recla,
Nine-Year-Old Entrepreneur

*To Mommy and Daddy for teaching me entrepreneurship
and letting me choose who I want to be.*

*To Bubba and Sissy for being the best
big brother and sister EVER.*

*To Kali for giving me lots of furry love
and reminding me to play.*

*And to all the parents who have the courage to inspire
their kids to be young entrepreneurs.*

This is for you.

Contents

Acknowledgments

I started this book when I was seven. Now, I'm nine. At the beginning, I had no idea what it takes to write a book. Now that it's done, I'm very, very glad I did it. If you've ever thought of being an author, know that things might not always go the way you thought, but at the end of the day, it's worth it.

I learned quite a few things, like:

- Writing a book takes patience.
- It's okay to change my mind.
- It takes a tribe to write a book.

There were so many people in my tribe, and I'd like to thank you all!

Thank you, Mommy and Daddy, for all the help with this book. I'm very thankful that you were there for every step of the process.

To Keith and Maura Leon with YouSpeakitPublishing, thank you for this opportunity. And a very big thank you to Karen Burton for holding my hand in this process and for being very patient as I decided what I was going to say. I would never have finished this book without you.

A special thank you to the Gronich family: Ari, for suggesting that I write this book, Shannon, for always supporting and loving me and creating the Business Acceleration Summit where I won the pitch tank, and Gabriel, for giving the best hugs and being the best CEO Space little brother EVER.

To my CEO Space family, I am who I am today because you supported me and helped me grow. I mean, what event lets a two-year-old run around handing out her own business cards?!? Let's hear a HUGE round of applause for CEO Space; you'll always be in my heart.

To the Dohrmanns—Uncle Berny and Auntie September—thank you. You mean so much to me, and this book would never be like this without you.

To Ross Snyder, I will never ever forget what you did for me. Thank you so much for having the courage to put a seven-year-old, whom you didn't know, on stage as the capstone keynote of your largest event. When I stepped out in front of over two thousand people for my very first talk EVER, it was so inspirational and awesome to know I was being heard by all those people. Thank you for helping me find my passion and share my message.

To Kolby Kay, you're awesome! You took a chance on a seven-year-old by putting her on your stage at Meltdown in the Desert. You helped me get my first sponsors and deliver a kick-arse introduction at my very first keynote. You rock!

To Greg Reid, thank you for inviting me to speak at Secret Knock and for supporting young entrepreneurs.

To Steve Olsher and Kelly Poelker with New Media Summit, thank you for believing in me and inviting me to be an *Icon of Influence*. And a really big thank you for having an awesome DJ and dance floor and creating an event where I made so many great friends.

To Afrin and Iman Khan, thank you for helping me get clarity about my message by asking me that one important question, "What pisses you off?"

To all my sponsors: The idea of a seven-, eight-, or nine-year-old kid writing a book for parents about business is kind of insane. What's even more insane is the same kid getting sponsors for that book. It was challenging for me when people said *no* to my project and told me that it didn't make sense for a business to support a kid writing a book. You heard me, and you believed in me. Thank you for making this possible:

Tonya Dawn Recla with *Super Power Experts*

Justin Recla with *Clear Directory*

Kathy Wells with *Prosperity Jumpstart Bootcamp*

Claire's Place Foundation

Marty Ward with *Confidence Eliminates Bullying*

Valorie Hubbard with *Actor's Fast Track*

Karen White and *Chateau 20*

Natalie Perkins with *Bella Ballerina*

Jeffrey Goodman with *Career Hearted*

Joseph Caldwell with *Consolidated Assurance and First Responder Benefit Association*

Tyler Harris with *The Daily Bread*

Viki Winterton with *Expert Insights*

Keith and Maura Leon with *YouSpeakIt Books*

To my Neva fans: You heard me too. Each of you supported me and this book. I am so grateful that you're part of my tribe:

Grandma Wiley

Jack and Becky Recla (Papa and Nana)

Dean and Nancy Banz (Papo and Nanny)

Bruce Goldwell

Callie Kron

Judy Feldhausen

Rita Paulino

Debra Graugnard

Marilyn Macha

Chris Salem

Geri Burke

Bonnie Laslo

Karen Doerflein

Shane Lanning

Mike Rudge

Drew Berman

Dawn Gluskin

Carrie Jeske

John Fitch

Finally, to all my family and friends who have supported me over the years, thank you and I love you.

Little Stories About Neva

The question we get asked the most is, "How did Neva happen?" or some version of that. Of course, the obvious answer never suffices because what people really want is for us to explain the inexplicable. They want a story they can wrap their minds around to make sense of the magic and mystery that is our daughter. It doesn't exist. There is no way to understand something like this. Because after the typical parental pride and bias end, the undeniable truth begins that she is here to invite us to perceive beyond ways we previously perceived, to challenge our faith beyond typical spiritual growth or woo-woo mantras, and to model a way of beingness that requires us to step into the highest and best versions of ourselves. Of course, she does "normal" kid things. Of course, she plays with toys, occasionally doesn't clean her room, and sometimes argues about doing her learning. But rest assured, she knows things we can't comprehend and lives so purely in her purpose that we can only strive to follow. We live with her and still live in awe of her. And this is only the beginning.

Justin and Tonya Dawn Recla,
Founders of the Super Power Experts® and
Clear Business Directory™

Neva is not only my spirit animal; she's also a bright light that shines inspiration on all around her. Neva's playful spirit with her drive to succeed is a winning combination for people of all ages to learn from. I'm very grateful to know Neva!

JP Sears, @AwakenwithJP, Author of
How to Be Ultra Spiritual

The future couldn't look more bright when you have a powerful soul like Neva holding the helm for our youth. Our first encounter enveloped me with love and admiration and has only grown from there over the years. We have shared stages in front of thousands, and there is never a dry eye as Miss Neva's story and power move people to action. It is an absolute honor to call her and her family part of my own. This book will give you direction, hope, and a plan to take your dreams to the next level.

Kolby Kolibas, Author and Founder of the
Meltdown in the Desert Event Series

I've watched Neva over the years navigate various business conference environments. From an early age, it was obvious she not only belonged in them but is here to impact them. I've had the honor of watching her speak on the Secret Knock stage and witness, first hand, the powerful impression she makes on an audience. If you have a stage, put her on it. If you have a chance to experience her on stage, through her podcast, or in this book, do yourself a favor and listen to what she has to say.

Dr. Greg Reid, Author, *Think and Grow Rich* series and founder of Secret Knock

Being a witness to the astonishing growth and impact Neva is making on the world around her is nothing short of inspiring. Her awareness of her world and how she navigates in it sets an example of how to move through life with ease, excitement, and curiosity. Big things are in store for her big spirit, and it is truly an honor to be a part of it; even in the smallest of ways.

September Dohrmann, CEO and President of CEO Space International

Neva is absolutely adorable! She is a legit BOSS. She works so hard and has such an amazing entertainment career ahead of her. She is definitely one to watch!!

Rachel McCord, Founder of The McCord List Institute for Fashion, Entertainment, and Influence in Hollywood, California

When I first met Neva, I knew I was in the presence of a master! Neva is one of the most amazing and natural leaders I've had the pleasure of connecting with. Don't let her age fool you. She is

a natural leader and intuit. Her vision and calling of purpose is strong and her light is bright and shines on all who cross her path. As an authentic entrepreneur from the very start, she is engaging, well-spoken and a true visionary! Neva is more than just our future generation; she is our hope for all she stands for in the world. I am honored to know such an incredible young lady, and if you ever have the chance to experience her presence, you are a fortunate individual! Neva brings authentic essence, energy, and passion to all she does!

Dame Shellie Hunt, @ShellieHunt, Recipient 2015 Lifetime Achievement Award - The White House, Founder of Women of Global Change & Success is By Design

Neva Lee Recla has accomplished more in the nine years of her life than many people accomplish in a lifetime. When I first met Neva at a networking event, she reached out her hand and, as she shook mine, she said, "Nice to meet you, I'm Neva." She was two. That was the beginning of one of the most special relationships in my life. She has been my friend, my mentee, my teacher, and my client. She hired me to represent her by taking me out to high tea at the Phoenician Resort. After a debate with her mom, she finally conceded that I could drive us to the meeting (she wanted to have me picked up by a service), but she insisted on paying. Neva is beyond inspiring. She knows what she needs to accomplish in each of her business ventures and speaking engagements, she seeks assistance from advisors and mentors for planning, and then she executes beautifully. To watch her on stage is inspiring. It's not surprising that the audiences are impressed at how well she speaks for her age. But for Neva, the audiences are impressed with her persuasiveness and power without regard to her age. Her skills rival those of adult motivators. This book is just another in a long series of impact-filled ventures accomplished by this young entrepreneur. I am proud to be Neva's lawyer, and I am honored that she asked me to contribute this input.

Maria Crimi Speth, shareholder with the AV-rated firm, Jaburg Wilk. Recipient of Top 100 High Stakes Litigator, Recognition of Excellence by Litigation Council of America, 2017 Women in the Law Best Lawyers

I have had the privilege to know Neva for a couple of years and was honored to feature her as an "Icon of Influence" at The New Media Summit. Few adults I know have her poise, conviction, ability to communicate clearly, and drive. I cannot wait to witness her continued growth and the inevitable impact she will have on the world. Young people of all ages should heed her advice, follow her lead, and live by the exemplary example of strength, conviction, and passion she demonstrates.

Steve Olsher, Creator of
The New Media Summit and
New York Times bestselling author of
*What Is Your WHAT? Discover the ONE
Amazing Thing You Were Born to Do*

I've had the honor of watching Neva at various business conferences over the years, including my own. I've also gotten to spend time with her personally and one thing is clear about her—she's always who she is, no matter the setting. Her ability to move and impact an audience rivals the most seasoned speakers. Her ability to connect at a one-on-one level and tune in to what people are dealing with is inspirational. Neva's drive, spirit, kindness, and playfulness make her a unique and refreshing voice in today's market, and I can't wait to see what else unfolds for the world from her.

Iman Khan, President, Red Elephant

The moment I met this little earth angel, she had my heart. I have watched her mentor and inspire thousands. Neva has a way of miraculously bringing people to life and connecting them as she sprinkles her pixie dust. She inspires with her art and youthful clarity. Neva, at six years old, was the winner of our Business Acceleration Pitch

Tank, competing with mature adults. Some would say she is an old soul . . . advancing through life at an accelerated pace. Neva is not to be missed.

Shannon Gronich, @ShannonGronich,
Creator of the Dare to Live Challenge
and Business Acceleration Network

I have worked with Neva Lee Recla since age two. Neva is an exciting Generation Z lady leader who has impressed people in her ventures since age four. She has worked with Jack Canfield, Bob Proctor, Sharon Lechter, Greg Reid, and thought leaders with over one billion followers. We have all poured lessons into Neva. Today as Neva advances her books, television projects, and movie deals into her future, we who mentor her have moved from "impressed" to STUNNED. Neva has elevated her game like a Zuckerberg or Larry Paige, with values, ethics, and integrity that is off all the charts. Neva's intuitive leadership keeps her leading edge. In places like Burning Man and in our own CEO Space International clubs, Neva is sought out for her guidance and advice. Her teaching and learning capacity stuns everyone and is an example of the PROMISE AND HOPE our upcoming generations promise to us all. GO NEVA.

Berny Dohrmann, Bestselling Author/Producer and
Founder of CEO Space International.

Prologue

It All Started With a Pig

"I want to make a million dollars like you."

Why?

"It sounds like fun."

What will you do with a million dollars?

"Hmm . . . I want to buy a pet pig."

That's awesome! What will the pig look like?

"He will be black with white spots."

And what will you name him?

"Hamlet. Hamlet Chicarrones Recla."

This was part of a conversation I had with Liz Benny at an event called *Meltdown in the Desert*. When I talked to Liz, I felt like she got me. During our conversation, she told me, "Neva, it's okay to want to buy a pig and to want to make a million dollars."

I started doing business when I was two years old, and now I'm nine. I'd always wanted to make a difference, and giving is important, but after this conversation, I realized that I didn't always have to give. I could make a difference and want to reward myself at the same time.

The reason I started business when I was two years old was because I saw all these adults around me doing business and being good at it. I thought, "If these adults can do it, why can't I?" I wanted to get a taste of the entrepreneurial life. But I wanted to do it my way. The rebel way. The imperfectly perfect way. The kid way.

I want to change the world. And I want to show other kids they can do whatever they want to do. One of my mottos is:

> I believe all kids have super powers, and we can change the world.

I really, truly believe that. But we can't change the world if we do what everyone tells us we're supposed to do. We can't change the world if we try to act like we don't like to play or dream or buy things or adopt pets or have fun or be ourselves.

When Pigs Fly

When I said I wanted to make a million dollars, Liz didn't tell me I was crazy or that kids can't make a lot of money. She just wanted to make sure I really knew why I wanted a million dollars. The conversation we had that day helped me name the book *When Pigs Fly*. My mom and dad and I sat down to brainstorm the title. We were looking for something fun that shows what I believe.

My parents told what this phrase meant—it means *anything is possible*—and I decided I really liked that. *When Pigs Fly* definitely sounded fun, and I do believe that anything is possible.

Plus, I want a pet pig, and I'm pretty sure pigs are going to fly one day.

The other important thing Liz told me was that it's okay to want things for myself. It's okay to want to buy a pig. At first that sounded selfish. But then my parents helped me see that by following my dreams, I could inspire other kids to follow their dreams.

I'm excited to share my book with you because I know there are other kids out there like me. I know, being the amazing parents you are, that you want to inspire your kids to follow their hearts. This book can help. I hope you enjoy it.

Love, Neva

Neva Lee Recla
9 years old
Phoenix, Arizona
February 2019

Introduction

The Beginning

It all started when I was two years old. That's when I began my business adventures. My parents left their jobs working for the government and became entrepreneurs. I saw that they had business cards, and I wanted some of my own.

The conversation went like this:

Me: Hey, Mommy, hey, Daddy, can I have my own business cards?

Mommy: No, honey.

Me: B—b—but why?

Daddy: Because, honey, business cards are only for adults.

Me: Why?

Mommy: (shrugging her shoulders and making a confused face) I don't know. Do you? (asking Daddy)

Daddy: No, I don't know either.

And that's how I got my first business cards.

I didn't have a business at first—I just liked having cards. I went to networking events with my parents and handed them out. By the time we joined a group called CEO Space International, I was already a pro at shaking hands and meeting people. One of the members of the group gave me a whole bag of Italian glass bracelets and told me I could sell them and keep the profits. I sold them for twenty dollars apiece.

The bracelets were beautiful and people wanted to buy them. I learned that business could be easy, and I really liked making money. My parents let me take a percentage of the profits and buy whatever I wanted. After that, I knew I wanted to keep doing business.

My Many Businesses

After that, I had many different businesses.

At four years old, I started drawing pictures and selling them. Then my sister, Danica, and I became Jamberry consultants and called our business *Deva Jams*.

At five years old, I wanted to do something for veterans because both of my parents were in the Army, and I really wanted to thank veterans for their service. So, I used my drawings to start a business I called *Spreading Light, Love, and Pixie Dust*.

At six years old, I formed my own advisory board for a business called *Hot Clothes for Kids*. Wow, that was something! I got a lot of backlash because I was a kid using the word "hot" in her business name. And some adults thought that my outfits were inappropriate because I liked to show my belly. Even though some people didn't agree with me, I kept on going and did what I wanted to do.

I also did promotional videos and product reviews for other businesses. I even did a video for Bob Proctor's Stick Person Theory. That was fun!

At seven years old, I started *Super Power Kids*. It's like my mom and dad's business, *Super Power Experts*. I host a podcast and get to interview a lot of cool people like JP Sears, Liz Benny, Sean Stephenson, and Joe Polish. I also started this book project and began getting sponsors.

And now, at nine years old, I'm finishing this book that you're reading right now.

I know it might sound weird that I like doing business and that I've kept doing it for the last seven years, but this is what I like to do. Of course, I also like playing. I like watching my iPad, swimming, playing with my dog, doing ventriloquism, and just being a normal kid. But doing business is part of my normal.

Even though this may sound weird to some people, weird *is* my normal.

My Why

Along the way, a lot of people have asked me, "Neva, why do you want to do business?"

Sometimes I answered, "It's just something I like to do," but I've realized it's more than that.

My parents took me to an event called *Speak to Impact Live* put on by Red Elephant. It was a three-day event to help people find their message and learn how to speak it. During that event, we did a lot of amazing exercises that taught me how to speak and to teach people my message.

At first, I didn't know what my message was, but then this happened: One of the exercises in the workbook asked a very serious and important question:

What pisses you off about the world?

Note: I'm not really allowed to use that word nor am I really that comfortable saying it. But my parents and I decided it's okay if I use it here. And I think that because the people at Red Elephant are freakin' awesome and had the courage to use that word, it triggered a reaction deep inside of me that helped me realize my mission.

As soon as my mom and I read that question, I looked at her and wondered if I could actually say what I felt. I'd never really thought about it before, but in that moment, reading that question, I felt like I had a bull inside of me that was going to start charging any minute. I felt enraged by all the things that really tick me off about the world.

And before I knew it, that bull came out:

- The KKK
- Criticism
- Racism
- Judgement
- Litter
- When People Don't Take Responsibility
- When People Hurt Other People
- When People Hurt Animals
- When People Hurt the Environment
- When People Try to Boss Me Around Thinking They're in Charge of Me

After I finished my list, I took a deep breath. For the first time in my life, I realized I wanted to change the world.

CHAPTER ONE

The ABCs

Parents, after that bull charged out of me, I knew that I was here to make a difference. I'm here because I have a purpose in life. I am here to change the world. I know that kids are more than just people who go to school, play, and do what we're told. We are much more than that. We can change the world and, trust me, we will. But, parents, we will need your help.

It Starts With Parents

We have to start with our parents. I do want to inspire one million kids to do business, but I'm going to need some help. I'm going to need some backup. I know that you parents are going to be a big help because you know what your kids are passionate about. You know that they're amazing. You know they're beyond-words-amazing.

That's why I want your help—to teach these amazing kids that, no matter what they're passionate about, whether it's about being an astronaut, or dancing, or doing art, they can turn that into a business. They can teach other people what they're passionate about and how they can follow their hearts and follow their dreams. And then, *those* people can teach others, and it can go on and on. That's why I need your help.

The other reason I'm speaking to parents is because for kids to do business, they need support from their parents. Most kid environments don't encourage business, so a lot of kids don't think about it. But once they find out about business, a lot of kids love the idea and want to get started. Most of them don't know how or are scared to. Some of them hear from adults that it's not possible.

All kids have different things that inspire them. Some kids like art, some kids like dance, some kids like helping animals, and some kids like to make their own video games. All these ideas can become businesses.

Of course, not all kids want to do business, but I believe that it's important for kids to know that they *can* do business, even if they don't want to. Because the more we tell kids that anything is possible, they more they'll believe in themselves and have the courage to do what they want.

Believe in Your Kids
In addition to supporting their kids, parents must also believe in their kids. I know that I could not have started my businesses if I didn't have the support of my parents— knowing that they believed in me, they truly knew what I was capable of, and that I was here to make a difference and change the world. They never told me I couldn't do it.

They never said that it's impossible. They just said, "You got this!"

They had my back. Even when I got criticized for putting the word "hot" in my business name, even when people said a kid could never do business, my parents were always there for me. They were more than willing to look outside the box and to try and think *my* way about different business ideas.

> *Not only do parents have to believe in their kids, but they also have to believe their kids are capable of things that may not have been done before, things that the parents haven't done before either.*

My parents didn't run businesses when they were kids, and they didn't know any kids doing business, but they still believed in me. Even when they didn't know how I was going to do something, we worked together to figure it out. For kids to do business and impact the world, they must know that their parents believe in them too.

One of the most frustrating things I hear is when parents find out that I'm making a difference and changing the world and they respond by judging their own kids. Some parents say, "My kids suck! They can't do that."

That discourages me. When parents say stuff like that about their kids, it makes me feel like I don't want to do what I'm doing. I realize how lucky I am to know that my parents never say things like that behind my back. They just believe in me.

I know that these negative words come from the parents really just judging themselves when they see how my parents are parenting me. I know it comes from a place of scarcity and ego. It can be so hard to accept that you're insecure about yourself that it becomes easier to make it about your kids.

For me, when I want to blame my parents for something, I know that it's coming from my ego. I understand that. I know it will make me feel much better, much more loving and connected, if I talk to myself and say, "Does this feel good to me? Or am I just insecure about myself and making it about them?" Then I realize that I shouldn't blame my parents. I know they believe in me. I will feel better if I try harder to be the most loving person I can be in my family.

In order for kids to do business, they have to know that you believe in them and they have your full support and love.

The Five Steps
After I realized that I'm here to change the world, inspire kids to do business, and help parents, I came up with five

steps parents can follow to support their kids. I call them my ABCs because they're easy to remember and they're fun. These steps outline the things my parents did to support me on my business journey. They'll help you know what environments to look for, how to help kids be creative, and how to encourage them to have fun in business.

Here are the five steps:

- Adult Environments
- Being Included
- Choice
- Dream
- Excitement

Because this is a lot of information (and I'm nine!), my parents and I came up with questions for each section for them to ask me. I put my answers in each section. This makes it easier and more fun to read.

In each chapter that follows, you'll get advice from me in each of these five areas. I'll tell you about my experiences, and I'll tell you what I've learned from them. I have advice for parents, as well as advice for kids, whether they are just starting to think about business or are already young entrepreneurs.

Let's get started on those ABCs!

CHAPTER TWO

Adult Environments

Parents, if your kid wants to do business, it's critical that you take them into adult environments. This is a "need-to-happen" or else—let me tell you something—your kid's not going to be able to do business. You know how teachers teach kids how to do math, and how to do science at school? In the same way, business leaders and business events teach people how to do business and how to do it the right way.

Benefits of Adult Environments for Kids

There are many benefits for kids spending time at adult business events. If your kid goes to an adult environment, they will see people networking, shaking hands, handing out business cards, and talking to each other. They'll hear them saying, "Hey, I do *this*, if you're interested, let me know. Here's my card." Just being there watching will help kids get in the mindset of how to network. That's very important if you're going into business. You need to be able to get your business out there, and networking is key.

It will also teach them how to "speak" business. It really is like a secret language and they have to know how to speak it. You have to learn how to say what you mean without rambling on about other things.

Being at business events will teach your kid what to do and what not to do. If your kid already wants to do business, these events will let them see adults doing it. If they aren't sure, they can spend some time in these adult environments, and they might say, "Wow, I love what they're doing, it's so cool. It's amazing even. I want to do that, I want to be like that."

So, if you are a parent and you're going to a business meeting or a business event, consider bringing your kid. You could say to your kid, "Hey, are you interested in coming along? I asked if you could come if you are interested. Would you like to join me?"

And if they say, "Really? I can go with you?" then you should say, "Yeah, but you have to be willing to network and not play video games or play with dolls (or whatever your kid is interested in)." Let them know that they have to stay focused. You could say, "As long as you're focused and you're talking with people and you're telling people what you're interested in, they're more than happy to let you come."

My Favorite Environments

I've been lucky. I've visited with business people in lots of adult environments and have attended many events. When

I think about it, all my favorite adult environments have had one thing in common: an amazing community. Each of them is made up of a community of people who love and support each other. They've got each other's backs—even if they don't know each other very well.

CEO Space

One of my favorite adult environments has got to be *CEO Space*. I basically grew up there. It's where I learned how to shake hands, to hand out business cards, and talk to people about business. I first went there when I was two. It's an amazing environment. The reason I'm saying this is because pretty much everyone there believed in me. They didn't have a single doubt that I could change the world. They gave me advice on how I could change my SNAP, which I'll talk more about in a moment. They *scouted* for me, which I'll also explain later. People at CEO Space treated me like I was an equal and like I was amazing.

I know it's because of CEO Space that I'm who I am now. They gave me love, and they all supported me. They also let me give them advice, which was awesome. It was amazing because they treated me like I was one of them, like I was an adult, not a nine-year-old child.

What does *SNAP* mean? Well, SNAP is CEO Space's word for an elevator pitch. I don't remember what the letters stand for but it has a very exact meaning.

What do I mean by *scouting?* Well, if you meet with someone about your business and they're not a good fit for you as a business partner or book sponsor or something like that, then you might say to them, "Okay, I'll scout for you," and that means, "Okay, I'll look for people to help you find someone who is a good fit. I'm committed to helping you, and if I find someone, I'll bring them to you so you can have a good business partner."

You're never rude or snarky. You just say, "I'll scout for you," and that helps them feel accomplished. That way, they don't feel like you're saying, "Oh, I don't want to hang out with you. I don't want to be your business partner." At CEO Space, that's letting that person know, "I'm going to support you. I don't care if other people are judging you. I love what you're doing. You might not be a good fit for me, but I'm going to find someone who loves what you're doing just as much as I do, someone who's a great fit for you."

Other Favorites

I've listed some of my other favorite environments below:

New Media Summit. I met amazing people there, like JJ Flizanes, Doug Sandler, and Steve Olsher.

Eliances. I love Eliances. I just spoke there recently at the GRANDtable, and it was so cool. They have gifts that they give to everyone. David Cogan, the founder, always shares stories about his kids and his kids are normally there. Those gifts are actually based on what the kids wanted to happen. I learned from Eliances about the importance of the community and to always have your friend's back, even if it's someone you just met. Support each other, love each other, and be nice.

Red Elephant. Red Elephant is amazing. It's where I talked about what ticks me off about the world, and trust me, I went on and on. At a Red Elephant event called *Speak to Impact,* which was hosted by Iman and Afrin Kahn, I learned to craft my message, to know how I want to inspire a million kids to do business.

Meltdown in the Desert, hosted by Kolby Kay. I learned there that you have to keep going no matter what other people say.

Fast Inc. Network. I met Daymond John and Joe Polish and what I learned there was that, at the end of the day, people are just people. I remember I got a selfie with Daymond John. That was awesome.

Burning Man was hosted by thousands of people. I learned about radical self-expression and to just have fun, be wacky, be weird—that's a huge compliment in my house—and be *you.* Love yourself. Love other people too, and be nice.

CEO Space, hosted by Berny and September Dormann. I've already talked about CEO Space a bit in this book. I learned so much there about how to do business: how to shake hands, how to kiss babies, how to talk to people, and hand out business cards.

Business Acceleration Network hosted by Shannon Gronich. I did a pitch there at an event called Pitch Tank, which was like Shark Tank. I learned there how to do a pitch. And I won!

Learning From Adults

What do I learn from hanging around adults?

Watching them helps teach me who I want to be. For example, on one side of me, I might see people who are super happy and energetic. I talk to myself and I say, "Do I want to be like that? Yes. Okay, I'm going to start being more happy and energetic."

Then on the other side, there may be people who are sad and sarcastic. They're snarky to each other. They're mad almost all the time, like they have an icky energy to them. I talk to myself and I say, "Does this sound good? Do I want to be that person? No. Okay, then I'm going to manifest not seeing that many people like that in my life because I don't want to be like them. I'm not going to resonate with them, so why should I talk to them?"

Some other people are super energetic. They're happy, they're leaders, and, when they talk, they have a point. I ask myself, "Do I want to be like these people? A thousand times, yes. I'm going to manifest more of these people in my life."

Sometimes I find judgmental people around me. Oh my gosh, it can be hard to love myself when people are so critical. There've been quite a few times when I've judged myself because people have judged me.

> *I've actually learned from people who've been sarcastic and rude to me.*

I've actually learned from people who've been sarcastic and rude to me like the adults who criticized me about my *Hot Clothes for Kids* business. I've learned from these judgmental people. People are going to criticize me, but they play a role in helping me to learn to love myself even more and more and more. I don't give in to the stories. I don't say, "Oh, I suck because this one person hates me."

In my life, I know I might run into judgmental people sometimes, but there will always be people who believe in me, who love and support me. I talk to myself and I say, "These people are supporting me and as I more and more love myself, more of those loving people are going to come up in my life."

My Advice for Kids

The advice I would give to kids who want to be in adult environments is to learn from them, but to know when it's time to play, to run around and have fun, and to color, and sing and dance. Know when it's time to do business, and know when it's time to sit still, and be quiet, and listen. These are not times to doodle, and sing *lalala* because—let me tell you something—people aren't going to accept that.

There are occasionally times at business events when people take breaks to have fun. At New Media Summit, they had a dance floor once, and they had a DJ named DJ Doug. There was a bunch of music, the dance floor was lit up, and then everyone went back to business. When these fun things are happening, you need to know that eventually, people are going to say, "Okay, we need to go back to work now."

When I go to these events, what I do is observe how people are acting, and I try to act like them, so I don't get kicked out of the event. For example, if I see that people are quiet and not speaking, if I see them just listening and taking notes, I do the same thing. I don't mess around. I would say observe your environment. Feel into the energy of it, and if it feels like a good time to play, and sing, and dance with people, go ahead, but if it feels like a time to be quiet and listen, do that.

A Kid at the Grownup Table

When my parents left government, they made a pact that they weren't going to do anything business without me because they wanted to create a life that we could live together. We wouldn't have to leave each other. They wouldn't have to go work and speak without me. We could be together all the time.

Their business cards inspired me to want my own, and, after I got my own cards, I learned how to talk to people the way the adults did. CEO Space helped me a lot and that's why I talk about them so much. I learned to hand the business cards out at events. After a while, they realized I needed a business for those cards, didn't I? As I've already told you, I got my first business from CEO Space when a friend handed me a bag of Italian glass bracelets and he said, "You can sell them and keep the profits." That was my first business. It was amazing.

Someone asked me what it's like to be with adults in these environments. Do I feel like a kid at the grownup table? That's an interesting question. To me, it actually feels like I have a chance to be myself in that environment. That's one of the reasons why I love talking with adults. There are quite a few kids I literally don't get. I just don't speak their language.

On the other hand, I was talking earlier with my mom and I said, "I speak kid," and that's true too. I do speak kid, and I love talking to kids who are doing business. They're mature but they're kids, too, so I can just bring 'em and ramble so they get me. But there are other kids who are just messing around all the time, and I don't get them. When I see them, I'm like thinking to myself, "What the heck are you doing?"

So being with adults is almost like a chance to be myself again, you know. When I'm with adults, sure, sometimes I'm quiet, but I normally like engaging and I say a lot. I'm a people person, so if there are people who speak my language and they get me, if they understand me and they treat me like an equal, I'm going to like hanging out with them for the entire day. I guess I am literally a kid at the grownup table at the adult business events, but I usually feel comfortable. It's fun.

Kids in Business Need Adults

> *There are really no kid environments that talk about business.*

The reason I think it's important for kids to hang out in adult environments if they want to do business is because there are really no kid environments that talk about business. Kid environments usually try to program kids.

They say, "You have to act a certain way. You have to be a 'regular kid.'"

I actually have a story about this from my life that I remember very clearly. It was from when I was in kindergarten, and I was five or six at the time. They gave us this paper, a sheet with instructions on how to draw Mona Lisa. So, I did it. Well, I tried to do it, and when I was done, I gave it back to the teacher, and the teacher said to me, "It needs to look like *this*," and she pointed at the other papers.

I look back at that day, and I think to myself, "Why'd they try to get a six-year-old to draw that piece of art?" Looking back at that now, I also realized they were programming all of us kids to act a certain way, to all be the same.

I think there are also adult environments that program you to act a certain way. They teach you how to act like an adult or like people you would assume to be an adult. And some of them will help to teach you how to do business.

What I would say is, just go into the adult environments that feel resonating, the ones that feel uplifting. Choose the ones that help you move in the direction that you want to go, whether they're talking about business or they're talking about other things you want to learn to do.

CHAPTER THREE

Being Included

To all you parents reading this, my advice to you is to include your kids in your life as much as possible. It will teach your kids very important life skills like making decisions. That's an important one. It'll teach them how to cooperate with their friends and with their family. It will teach them how to think about what to do in the world and how to act independently. They can learn how to make decisions by themselves.

When you include your kids in more and more of your life, this will also teach them how to include others and how to be nice. And that's really important in life. Learning to include others can also relate to business. If you have a business partner, it can help you cooperate and be nice to that business partner. It can help you learn to include business partners in business plans, like saying, "Hey, let's go speak here. Does that sound like a good idea?" Including others will help your kids develop strong communication skills.

Not Only in Business

Include your children around the house when it comes to household chores and home decisions. For example, let's say you're the parent, and you say, "Hey, I want to go get a bite to eat." Instead of just saying, "Hey, we're going to go *here*," you can say to your kids, "Where would you like to go? What sounds good to you?" Together, you can come up with a compromise so they feel like they're being included.

Ask them what their opinion is, because that's including them. That's what my parents do with me. They don't make the decision about what we're having for dinner, what we're having for lunch, or breakfast. They think about what they want, and they say, "This sounds good to me," and then they say, "Neva, what sounds good to you?" I tell them what I think.

I think it's really important not only in business—including them in business meetings and stuff like that—but also in choices at home. That's really big. Your kid feels like, Oh, I get to say something here. It's not my parents against me. It's me *with* my parents."

First Step

Kids and parents should try to understand each other's language.

My parents and I don't necessarily have to do that because we are lucky enough to speak the same language. We talk with each other and about each other, and we keep talking until we understand.

One thing you can do is try to treat your kid like they're an adult. Like talk to them the way you would talk to a friend of yours. Do you know what I mean? Treat them like they can make good decisions, and that's a good first step.

The Benefits of Including Your Kids

There are many benefits of including your kids. If you're doing business, you're going to need to make hard decisions. You're going to need to make some tough decisions. Trust me, I have. And if you don't learn how to do that in your daily life, you're not going to be able to do business. You're not going to get through it.

Now

A huge aspect of the world is being included. Include your kids in your daily life now. You can start simple. I know this doesn't sound very hard, but to start, kids can choose what they're going to eat. You can start today. Have them choose what to have for dinner.

Making decisions lets kids practice how to do it. If they don't know that they can make decisions for themselves, it will get them to think like, "Oh, I need to make these hard decisions in business. If I'm interested in business, how am I going to do it?" They will wonder, "How am I ever going to do business if I can't make decisions?"

Including your kids trains them in a bunch of ways. When parents include them in more things, it helps kids learn to cooperate, and it helps kids become confident that they can work with other people.

Later

Including your kids will teach the kids how to do things when they're older and they grow up and move out. It will teach them that they can make decisions if they're living by themselves. They can make important decisions, answering questions like, "Where am I going to live? What house am I going to buy? Am I going to rent a house or am I going to buy a house?"

They will have to decide what job to take. They will have to figure out, "Is this a good job for me? Is it not a good job for me?" Including your kids in decisions will help them in so many ways. I don't know when your kid's going to move out—let's say fifteen years. In fifteen years, the way you've included your kid will help them live by themselves. So, when that happens, your kids can feel like, "Oh, wow. My parents helped me so much because they included me. Now I can make decisions for myself and I don't need help."

How My Parents Include Me

I have lots of examples of ways my parents include me. As I already told you, if they want something for dinner they'll ask, "Hey, what do you want for dinner? What sounds good to you?" If they're going to the store, they'll say, "Hey, Neva, is there anything that sounds good to you that you need or want from the store?" And I will answer this or that. They might ask me something like, "What do you want to do today?" Maybe one of us wants to go in the pool, maybe I want to go to the park, maybe one of them just wants to chill out on the couch. We talk about different ideas, and then we make decisions together.

We definitely compromise a lot, and I really like that because we're working as a team and it feels really good. It's also good to know that parents support you and they're okay with the decisions you make. If parents try to work around what you want and what they want, and you make the choices together, everyone's happier.

Advice for Kids

The advice I have for kids who want to be more included is to tell you to remember, "No, you're not the only one in the situation."

You can ask for what you want, but it's very important to know that you're not the only one in the house. You're not the only person that matters. I don't know you, but you might have siblings, you might have grandparents, parents, and even cousins that are living with you, and each different person in your life has their own wishes.

Keep this in mind when you're talking to your family. If you want to be included, you have to learn how to include other people too. Say something like, "Hey. I have this idea that sounds really fun to me today. What would you guys like to do?" Include them, because they might have a different idea, and you have to be willing to compromise. You might say, "Okay. Maybe today we can do what you want to do and tomorrow we can do what I want to do."

I find that works with friends too, like with my friends and me. It helps us get along, so we don't fight. Say we're talking about what to do, and one of my friends says, "No, I don't want to do that. I want to do this," I'll be like, "Okay. I want to do this, so maybe we could do a little bit of what I want to do today and a little bit of what you want to do today and the rest tomorrow." Everything works better if you include each other and are willing to compromise.

Burning Man

My parents once had plans to go to a festival called *Burning Man*. They were originally just going to go by themselves, and a friend was going to watch me. It's about a one-week event. They asked me, "Does that sound fun to you? Do you want to stay home?"

I didn't want to stay home for a week with a friend without my parents. It's just not fun to me. So they said, "We got you a ticket. It's all yours if you want it." I thought to myself for a little bit. Did I want to go to *Burning Man*? It was a fourteen-hour drive, but I was interested. It did not sound fun to be alone for a week without my parents with only a friend and my dog. So I made my decision and said, "Yes. I want to go to the festival with you guys."

We went, and it was the best experience ever to have with my family. It was definitely a life-changing experience, and it only happened because my parents were willing to include me. They also knew how much it mattered that I made that decision for myself, instead of them making it for me.

Including Others

> *When you include your kids, you also help them learn to include others in their lives and in their businesses.*

You can help them by understanding that they wish to be heard too. You can ask them, "Hey, I'm going to go to this business meeting. Do you want to come?" You can also ask them household things, like what to have for dinner. You can talk to your kids about decisions, like saying, "Hey, I want to go get this for dinner. What sounds good to you?" And then come up with a compromise so that your kid feels heard, and you both get what you want.

I think that you have to think about how your kid thinks and acts because everyone is different. You can work on getting really tuned in to feeling the energy of the moment, so you can figure out, like, "What's a good question to ask here so that I'm including my kid, but I'm also heard?" It's not putting the other person's idea aside. It's combining two thoughts and coming up with a good idea.

If you want your kids to include others, I find the best time you can teach them about this is when a problem comes up between friends. This will happen a lot in a kid's life. There have been quite a few times when I fought with my friends because we were putting each other's ideas aside.

If your kids come to you and say, "Hey Mom, or Hey Dad, I was fighting with my friend because they were putting my idea aside, and I didn't like their idea," you have a chance to talk about including others. You could say in that situation—again feel into it—but something like, "Well, how'd that make you feel?" And once they answer, you can say, "Okay. Well, maybe next time you can say to your friend that sounds like a really fun idea, so maybe we can do some of your idea and some of my idea today, and we can do the rest tomorrow."

Don't forget that one of the best ways to teach your kid to include others is to include them. You can't expect your kid to automatically know how to include others. They need to learn from you.

CHAPTER FOUR

Choice

> *Kids need to experiment in a safe place.*

Parents, if you want to help your kids be successful in life and in business, you have to let them have choice. You have to let them learn how to make choices, and you have to let them learn about consequences of their choices. It's so important because in business and in life, people have to make those choices. They'll have to make some tough decisions and either way, whether it's a good decision or a "bad" decision, they're going to have consequences, no matter what. They need to know that that's okay, and it's just life. If you let them know that there are consequences, they will be more and more careful with the choices that they make.

Consequences can be scary for kids. When we make choices, a lot of us don't want to know what the consequences are because we're scared. We don't want to have to be angry or get sad because of the consequences. That's why kids need to experiment with these things in a safe place—like at home. When they feel safe, they can take their time considering choices and consequences. They can mold the situation around and feel what they want to do.

As your kids get older and older, they can keep learning about choice and consequences, so when they move out they know what to do. They will know how to make good choices and handle the consequences.

This is extremely important in business because in business we have to make decisions all the time. For example, you will have to decide whom you're going to work with, and then you'll learn the consequences of working with that person or not working with that person. You have to decide if you want to make changes along the way, and you'll learn the consequences of that. You might have a business for a while and get to a point when you have to decide to keep it or to start a new business. No matter what, you're going to have to make choices and be willing to deal with the consequences. So start now by guiding your kids in choices and letting them learn the consequences of their actions.

My Story

Well, I can tell you that choice played a humongous role in my business experience. Earlier in the book, I touched on starting my business, *Spreading Light, Love, and Pixie Dust*. I started this business when I was five. I'll share with you how that all came about and how important choice was in this business.

At every CEO Space event, they do a veterans' tribute in which they have all the veterans in the room go and stand in a line so everyone else can thank them for their service.

My parents are both Army veterans, and I saw them in line with all those other amazing people who risked their lives to make ours amazing.

I went up to my mom and I said, "Mommy, I want to do something to support them." I didn't know what. My parents helped me come up with some possibilities. They asked me, "Well, what do you like to do?"

I said, "I like to draw."

We came up with the idea of drawing pictures and writing poems. I thought that was a great idea. I love drawing, so it was a good choice for me. Each year, I drew a new picture, and we handed them out as a family on Veterans Day and at events I attended that had veteran tributes. For this business, not only did my parents let me choose what to do, they also let me choose the name: *Spreading Light, Love, and Pixie Dust*. It described exactly how I felt about what I was doing.

Ever since then, I've been handing out these pictures. Last year, I handed out over a thousand pictures with my sister and my parents, and it's been just a life changing experience from the first moment on. It was amazing, and it all came from my parents letting me make choices.

How You Can Help

There are steps that parents can take to let their kids have more choices. First, you definitely should guide them, especially if they're at an age where they're just learning to choose and make decisions. I don't suggest putting a bunch of choices on them because it can be very overwhelming sometimes. Just guide them.

For example, let's say you're going shopping for clothes, and your kid wants an outfit but doesn't know which one. You can give them two options. You could give them more, but it's important not to give too many to start with. Then say, "Oh, this would look good or this would look good. Which one do you like better?" So, then it's like they can decide but you're still helping them make the choice. As they get better at making choices, you can give them more options.

Choice and Consequences

So part of what kids need to learn about choice is the consequences of the choices that they make. There are bunches of choices you make in business, so it's important for you, as a parent, to teach your kids how to manage each choice and how to manage the consequences of that choice. I've definitely had a few consequences.

One of the greatest things my parents taught me at a very early age was how to ask for what I want and how to get what I want. For example, if we were at the store and I was throwing a temper tantrum because I wanted a toy, they taught me that this wasn't a good way to act by making the consequences clear. Obviously, I wasn't getting the toy that way.

Was that behavior getting me any closer to getting me a toy? No, it was pushing me away from it. So they helped me learn the consequences. A good part of why I'm as mature as I am now is because they taught me choice.

When we were at my grandma's house once, I used a little bit of makeup from my mom's brush, and I put it on my face. I opened the bathroom door and I said, "Mom, look, I'm getting tanner." I closed it and I put more on my face and I said, "Mom, look I'm even tanner now." And then I did it again and I said, "Mom, I'm even tanner now." And then she's like, "Uh-huh. Yeah."

And I wasn't fooling her so it wasn't a good idea of mine. My mom talked to me about telling the truth, even in silly situations. I learned from that that you shouldn't lie when you have a choice. My parents have helped me know that I can share things with them. I love sharing things with my parents; it's one of my favorite things.

Hot Clothes for Kids, as I talked about earlier, was a fashion business I created. I chose the outfits. My parents guided me, but they let me choose my outfits. One of the consequences of this choice was a lot of criticism I got, because of the name of the business and the outfits that I chose.

I knew many people didn't support those outfits. I didn't even know if my parents liked all of them, but they let me make that choice. I normally choose crop tops and pants or shorts and high heels. My parents did help me decide what was a good outfit, but they let me decide what I wanted to wear. I chose what I felt looked good on me, even though people were criticizing me every five seconds. Dealing with criticism wasn't always easy, as I mentioned before, but I was doing what I loved to do. It's definitely a good example of letting kids make choices and dealing with the consequences.

Benefits of Choice

Some of the benefits I've experienced in choice definitely came from my podcast. As I mentioned early in the book, I started my *Super Power Kids* podcast when I was seven, and my parents helped by guiding me. Ever since I first saw my mom doing podcasts, I thought it was amazing, and I knew I wanted to do it, too.

I didn't scream and whine about it. I asked her for what I wanted. I said, "Mom, what you're doing is amazing. Can I try it?" We strategized for months to come up with the right name and the right ideas, and finally, we came up with *Super Power Kids*. We do funny FaceTime and interview amazing people. It's so much fun.

Over the year that I've had the podcast, I've really made it my own. I had an idea, I made my choice, and my parents helped me with it. As a result, I now have the benefit of managing a really fun podcast.

Learning

The area of life where I think choice has played the biggest role for me is definitely my schooling. I've been to different schools, and I've been homeschooled. I've been able to make choices about my schooling with my parents' guidance.

When it comes to schooling, I feel free to tell my parents how I feel and ask my parents questions like, "Hey, is it okay if I go to this school?" They allowed that. They found schools for me that we all liked. Then I asked, "Hey, can I learn from home?" They accepted that too. I'm homeschooled now, and they have let me decide what curriculum I like. I love this homeschooling thing. I really enjoy it. And they like knowing that I like the decisions that we make as a family.

Part of the reason I love being homeschooled is because I don't have to leave my family. This has made me happier with my learning. I enjoy being able to wake up when I want to wake up. I enjoy being able to spend time with my family and not be away from them. I enjoy knowing that if I'm focused on learning, I get playtime. At other schools, I felt like I was trapped. At most schools, you have certain hours a day that you learn. Even if you work fast, you're still going to be there for that amount of time.

Making these choices about my schooling and having my parents' support has definitely helped me learn and be happy about learning.

Eating

Another good example I have about having choice is the food I eat. There were a lot of times when I went to my parents and said, "Hey, can I eat this? Hey, can I have this?" Then it got to the point where they realized it's my body. I am the one who has the sense of what it feels like to eat certain things.

At that point, they told me, "It's your body. Eat what you want to eat, but know that there are consequences to eating certain things."

I learned how my body responds to foods. There was one day when I ate ice cream. I just ate sugar that entire day. I went back to my parents and I said, "Ugh, I'm not going to eat sugar again," I was able to say that because I had learned the consequences of that choice. I felt sick to my stomach, and it wasn't a good feeling, so I learned to eat healthier.

Now, when my dad's like, "Hey, what do you want to eat?" he'll usually make me what I want to eat, or I'll go make what I want to eat. They let me have that choice.

Advice for Kids

The advice I have for kids who want more choice in their life is has three parts:

- Be willing to ask for what you want
- Take action
- Be flexible

For example, you probably remember that I wanted a pet pig. I'm still wanting him. I went and asked my parents, "Can I have a pig?" Their original answer was, "No."

So I took action. I was looking at pigs online, I was strategizing, and I was coming up with ideas. Finally, when I was ready, I went back to my parents, and I said, "When I make my first million dollars, is it okay if I have a pig?" And they said, "Yes." They agreed that when I made my first million dollars, they were going to step out and let me choose what pet I wanted. I said I definitely wanted a pig.

That was awesome because they let me choose what type of animal I wanted, and they didn't say *no* again. They were happy that I took action and was willing to be flexible, so they said *yes*. Now, they're helping me work up to that goal.

If I had pouted and gotten upset about getting a *no*, there is no way I would have gotten a *yes*. If I hadn't taken action, I wouldn't have gotten it. If I had been inflexible with my parents, I wouldn't have gotten a *yes* either. When you're not flexible, people will pick up on that energy, and they'll play a resisting role for you, so you don't get what you want until you work up to that action.

> *Remember to ask for what you want, take action, and be flexible.*

CHAPTER FIVE

Dream

Parents, if you really want your kid to be successful in business, if you want them to dream and really get in tune with that purpose that they are here to do, you have to dream yourself. You have to willing to be playful, and be loving, and be fun, and kind of represent that for your children so they can follow you. If I see my parents doing something, I know that it's safe and it's fun, because they're really playful with me like that.

If you're playful, if you're happy and joyful, if you do your best not to get irritated on this journey, you will do amazing things. Model your big dream for your kids. Maybe you have forgotten what it was like to dream when you were a kid. If so, maybe you can use this time with your child as a time to find your dream, and your purpose. Do it together, and use teamwork.

Remember to dream, to have fun, and to love each other.

Is Dreaming in Business Necessary?

I think dreaming is an important concept in business because if you don't dream, you're not going to have fun, and that's an important part of business to me. I think in order to create a business, you have to think about what you love to do. You have to dream about it.

If you are thinking about business, a good place to start is asking yourself, "What do I dream about?" Then make that dream into reality.

I can remember times I've dreamed and it's led to a business. As I've mentioned, after I saw my mom doing podcasts on *Super Power Experts*, I got interested in doing this myself. I started having a bunch of dreams and visions about me doing my own podcast, and that's how *Super Power Kids* came to be.

It was able to happen only because I started talking with my mom and my dad about my dream. We didn't know if we were going to do it, if we were ready to do it, how it was going to happen, or when. It was just a dream in the beginning, but we accomplished it, and I've been doing it for a year now.

I have some new dreams now. One of them is Hamlet, the pet pig I dream of having one day, after I make a million dollars. That's a big dream to have. I also dream of inspiring a million kids to get into business. Those are big numbers and big dreams, but I think if you have a dream and just set your mind to it, you can do it. Remember, anything is possible.

Kids and Adults: Different or the Same?

> *I think dreams depend more on the person than their age.*

Do kids dream differently from adults? Some kids might dream smaller than adults, but some kids might dream bigger than adults. There are so many ways to dream. A kid can dream of being a flight attendant, but so can an adult. You can dream of being a ballet teacher or a musician—I don't think it has anything to do with age really. Anyone can dream, no matter how old they are.

Sometimes I feel that adults can forget to be playful, and go into worrying about money and stuff. I feel like sometimes adults have been programmed to think about those things and live that way. Kids haven't had as much time to be programmed, so we might be a little more playful. Some kids, though, are more like adults than other kids, and some adults can be very playful. It all depends on the person.

Encouraging Kids to Dream

Parents can help encourage their kids to dream. My advice is first to find out what your kids like to do. Then ask them if they have a dream. If they already know what they want to be, like an entrepreneur or something, then ask them if they have any cool ideas. Then, I think, just take it from there.

One of the things we do is talk about *big ideas*. You can define a big idea as one that solves a big problem. I think something you could do is ask your kid, "What's your big idea?" That way, they can brainstorm good ideas, like coming up with solutions for problems in the world. They might already have a problem in mind that they want to fix. You can say, "Okay. So what's your big idea on how you can fix that problem?" After that, you can help them mold their ideas into possible solutions, so they can help others that might have that same problem.

You parents can model that process by telling your kids some big ideas you have, and talking about ways to make them happen. Maybe, let's say at mealtime, everyone can throw their big idea into the middle of the table. Maybe you can get a jar and have everyone in your family write a big idea and put them all in the jar. You can close your eyes and pick one of the ideas out of the jar. Someone can read it out loud and say, "Okay, how do we fix this?"

Finding Their Purpose

Everyone has a purpose in the world. It could be that not everyone agrees with that purpose. But they do have a purpose. Everyone has a purpose, but I feel that if you don't know your purpose, you won't accomplish it, so that purpose won't be met.

I feel like some kids already know what their purpose is. It depends partly on how in-tuned they are. If they are in-tuned and they are excited about it, I think they totally know. If they're not as in-tuned, then I think it may take them a little longer to know what their purpose is.

> *People get stressed out, and they feel like they're being choked.*

Sometimes I feel that people get stressed out, and they feel like they're being choked. I think figuring out your purpose can kind of loosen up the choking. I think that if people are stressing, they can feel better if they just have a dream. If they have a big dream that they want to accomplish, it can kind of help them loosen the reins and be more comfortable with doing what they need to do in the world.

This is true for adults or kids, whether they are entrepreneurs or not. If you have a dream set, like being a doctor, or an astronaut, or a ballet teacher, it will help you do what you need to do.

Finding Their Big Self

Dreaming can help kids figure out their purpose. I think this is because it helps show them who they really are. We kids sometimes have trouble figuring out who we are. Many adults also have trouble with this. If you have a big dream, a big idea to do something, or a problem to fix, it can be easier. Dreams help tie us back into who we are.

It can also help you get in touch with your *big self*. To me, your big self is like a higher self, and your little self is like a lower self—I think of it as my *whiny* self, to put it in kid words. Little selves pout all the time. They're kind of grumpy and they're not nice. Your big self is super nice, super energetic, and shows who you really are. Your big self is much more able to communicate because, while your little self whines, your big self *talks*.

Advice for Parents

The advice I have for parents who want to help their kids dream and get in touch with their purpose is be okay with them saying "No" at first. They might say "No" because they're scared to get in-tuned. But trust me; we kids come back around. Even if it takes you ten or twenty times, we will eventually come around and figure it out.

Just try your best to own up to what's yours and don't get frustrated, because if you get frustrated—trust me—it's going to be a whole lot worse. For me, if I know that my parents are frustrated, I'll be frustrated, and I won't cooperate because they're getting mad at me and they're getting frustrated, and I can't manage to go in as my higher self like that. So, be flexible and be loving, the loving parent that I know you are.

CHAPTER SIX

Excitement

Parents, you might be wondering how you can get your kids to do business if you know that they're passionate and excited about it, but they're scared and nervous and all mixed up.

First, focus on the fun and exciting things in business with your kids, because that'll make the not-so-exciting things in business look like fun too. Talk to them in their language, even if it's a make-believe language. When you're trying to get something across to them, talk to them in terms of what they're passionate about. For example, if they're passionate about trains, you can say, "You have to get the train to the station, you have to make sure it gets to its final destination." If they love doing ballet, you could say, "You have to nail this one, your last and final twirl."

So put it in a language that your kid can understand, and be fun about it. Don't be like, "You have to do this and that." Be happy about the process, but you have to actually be happy about it yourself, you can't just pretend to be happy because, trust me, us kids will pick up on it. We'll be like, "You're being sarcastic right now, parent." You don't want that.

Just be yourself. Be loving and be excited with your kid, and your accomplishments will be amazing for you both. It will also be great bonding time.

One of the great things I think kids bring to business is all their playfulness, excitement, and fun. They need to know that business is work, but it can be fun work. It's their choice, and yours, to bring out the fun. You can make it boring. You can make it a snooze fest. But you can also make it happy, all unicorns and rainbows.

Remind your kids that they have full control of how they manage their business. Remind them that they can choose to be sleeping, be bored, and thinking, "This sucks," but they can also choose to be thinking, "Oh, this is exciting, I'm so excited to do my business!" Let them know that they can choose to be excited and happy about it and tell all their friends, but they can also choose to pout. Give them choice A and choice B. Tell them which one's the more powerful side. Tell them that the power pose is the excitement and the weak pose, or the more villainy pose, you could say, is the choice to pout. But most importantly—this is to you, parents—it's so much easier for us kids to be excited about it if you're truly, from deepest down in your heart and from the very top, excited about it yourself.

It's easier for kids to be excited if you, our parents, are excited too.

76

My Own Experience

Excitement means to me being joyful and happy. Like, let's say you're excited about doing something creative. Like for me right now, I'm excited about finishing this book. Sometimes I have mixed feelings, and when someone asks me how I feel, I might say "nerd," which is a mix between nervous and excited. Kids have mixed emotions at times. You're excited. You're scared. You're happy. You're fearful. You're all these things at the same time, and it's like one big ball and you just have to throw it out there. It's helpful to keep focusing on being fun and playful.

I've experienced a lot of times when I've been excited in business settings, but I think one of the big ones was my first-ever talk to two thousand people. It was amazing. I was nervous, but I was super excited to share with all these amazing young adults what I was doing. For me, I think I am most excited when I am making a difference.

Another time I remember being super excited was when I met Daymond John from Shark Tank. He is known as the people shark. I'd been watching Shark Tank, and enjoying all the entrepreneur ideas that came on, and when I knew I might meet him, I was like, "Oh my gosh, we're going to meet Daymond John, I can't believe it!" I saw how many people there were. I looked through the whole line, and I finally saw him. Well, I was super excited, I was super nervous too, because I didn't want to mess up or anything.

But he actually walked over to my dad and said, "I will get a selfie with her".

I grabbed my mom's phone, and I walked into the meeting room. I hoped that he wasn't in a meeting, but he was just walking in. When I walked up to him, he grabbed the phone and took a selfie with me. It was amazing. I walked back to my parents, thinking, "I just got a selfie with a celebrity, oh my!" It was a really cool experience.

Fear and Excitement: The Connection

I do feel fear. I know people say a lot of the time that I'm fearless and I'm strong and I'm powerful, but like any human being—or alien—I feel fear. I get nervous, and I get excited, but I think the connection between nervousness and excitement matters. Sometimes you're excited because you're nervous. Sometimes you're nervous because you're excited. It makes a difference.

My parents surprised me when I finished third grade. They surprised me by telling me we were going indoor skydiving. I'd always wanted to try it, but once I get to that very moment where I was actually going to do it and go fifteen feet up in the air, I was nervous.

I was nervous, and I was excited, but part of the reason I was so excited is because I was a little nervous. Once I saw all the people going high and low and dancing around in the air tunnel, I got more and more excited. Sometimes there's something big that you want to do, and you might be nervous but tap more into the excitement and face your fears.

Trust me! It feels amazing after you face your fears. And if you're a little scared and you're not really sure about doing it, do it anyway. If your higher self is calling it, if it's calling your name, do it, and you'll have a blast knowing that you faced your fears.

Help Harness the Energy

Parents can help their kids harness their excitement to do something scary. If your kid is a little nervous, maybe because they're doing something for the first time, something new, talk to them about how exciting it sounds. Tell them you're proud of them, and help them feel more and more empowered, so they feel like "Oh, I got this. I can do it."

Sometimes, your kid may be super energetic. They might say, "Oh I want to do *this*. I want to do *this*. I want to do *this*." Say they have all these amazing ideas, and they're excited about all of them. Help them tie it back around to business. Maybe you can help them pick out the top three ideas, or the top two even, selecting good ones that can be hooked together to create a business.

Sometimes it takes time, patience, and willingness to work together. For example, *Super Power Kids* took months to put together. And it took us many, many months to figure out how I could help veterans with *Spreading Light, Love and Pixie Dust*. When your kids have a bunch of ideas, you have to be willing to teach them how to be patient, and you have to be patient yourself. Maybe it's going to take you two or three years, or even longer, but if your kid has a goal set, they will accomplish it, and you can help them.

Less Than Perfection

Even after you start a business, sometimes things don't work out right away. Parents can really help the kid entrepreneur at times like those.

Maybe your kid's first idea is kind of a flop. Maybe they start a YouTube channel and it doesn't get the million views they expected. Maybe they get some criticism that's hard to hear. Parents can help by telling them that it's okay. You can say, "You know what? It happens to everyone!" For example, like with a YouTube channel, if it doesn't get a lot of views, tell them, "It's okay. Just keep going if you love to do it."

When my mom, started *Super Power Experts,* she didn't do it to get a million hits. She did it solely because she wanted to do it and that helped her. Now she has a huge following. This doesn't mean that if you pretend to do something from your heart that you'll get hits. It has to be real. You have to start a business because you honestly want to start it.

You also want to help your kids set realistic expectations, but be supportive of their ideas at the same time. Like when they want to start a business, you can't tell them it's going to start immediately. But you also can't tell them, "You won't be able to do it." Tell them what you believe. If you believe that they can do it, tell them. If you believe that it might not work out in the first try, tell them. If you think they should consider some changes in their plan, tell them. Be honest, but set realistic expectations. Don't be like, "It's never going to work." But also don't be like, "It's totally going to work on the first try."

The Benefits of Excitement

Excitement can help kids get through the hard times of business. Sometimes, in business, you get criticized. If kids stay excited about their business and they are really truly happy, it's easier to keep going when you have hard times. When they get criticism, they can say, "You know what? Everyone's been criticized." They could even look at me for an example. Do you think that I stopped when I was being criticized by people for *Hot Clothes for Kids?* No. Because I loved doing it.

So if your kid is being criticized, you could tell them, "Look at Neva. She was doing *Hot Clothes for Kids,* and she got criticized, but she kept on going." As long as they stay excited and happy about what they're doing, all is well. You also can't expect that it's going to be all rainbows and unicorns all the time. You can be sure that it's going to be like that at the end, but know I don't mean it's going to be that way immediately.

My advice to kids is just keep on going. Keep on cutting down the hard vines and stuff, and you will get there. Stay excited, and it will help you get through the hard times and set realistic expectations for yourself.

One time, I was interviewed for an Inc. Magazine article. We were at Starbucks for the interview, and I had a Starbucks S'mores Frappuccino. While the reporter and I were talking about business and stuff, I said, "You can't expect that life's gonna be all S'mores Frappuccinos." That quote got featured in Inc. Magazine!

What I meant by that is that life's not always going to be sweet. It won't always be like the cherry on top. It won't always be all unicorns and sprinkles—but it will be, eventually.

Kids have to know that there's work involved. I love telling people I've been doing business for seven years, since I was two. Now I'm writing a book, creating a course, and doing a podcast. It takes a lot of work to get things done. I'm not just sitting around playing Minecraft on the couch all day.

The ideas for my businesses were mine, and they came from my dreams and my excitement. But the businesses happened because I was willing to do the work. If you aren't willing to work, business isn't for you. Remember that if you don't do the work, you don't get the right to brag. I like bragging. I like saying what I've done. If you like to do that then you need to work.

I love doing what I do, partly because it wasn't something that my parents did for me. It wasn't something my friends came up with. It was something I came up with. I had the ideas, and I did the work. That feels good. It keeps me excited and happy.

Walking Yourself Through the Feelings

Business can be stressful for adults and kids. I have had to deal with feelings like fear and excitement and nervousness and sadness. How do I manage my feelings? To be honest with you, my parents help me a lot. But I also use a kind of internal dialogue.

When I am struggling a bit, I ask, "Why am I feeling this way? What triggered this?" Once I figure it out, I normally talk to my parents and say, "Hey, I'm triggered about this," or "I'm a little nervous," or "I'm kind of excited," or "Hey, I'm sad about this." And that helps me. The internal dialogue helps me a lot just to figure out what's going on and what kind of talk I need to have with my body.

After that, talking out my feelings with my parents is very helpful.

If I'm going on stage in an adult environment, and I'm getting ready to speak or something, what helps me a lot is to move my body around. I'll do jumping jacks, or sing a little bit, or I'll just move my body. Sometimes, I'll just bring my leg up and down. That helps as well. I like to pace sometimes if I'm nervous.

I am in motion most of the time. I have to make sure that, on stage, I have room to walk around because with me, anytime I'm up, I'm walking. I have to walk, or I have to move some part of my body.

So also—this is for everyone—you have to realize there's a lot of energy in adult environments sometimes. You'll pick up on it. At events, sometimes, the speakers can be really loud, and they can yell. If there are energetic speakers at the event, you'll pick it up. It can be exciting, but it can also be stressful.

Really, you just need to find what helps you in that situation. Maybe it's something different every time. Maybe you're pacing one day, you're popping your knuckles the next. Maybe you're dancing or singing. Whatever. Just find what truly helps you to get through what you need to do. Some people have squishies or they have a stress ball that they squeeze to help relieve stress. Some people take breaks and listen to music, or watch videos on YouTube or something. Find something satisfying for you.

CHAPTER SEVEN

Raising a Young Entrepreneur

Parents:

So now that you know the ABCs of how to raise a young entrepreneur, it's time to talk about you and parenting. It's important that you have the courage to raise your kid differently—in a way that's unlike traditional parenting. If you know that your child is here to have an impact on the world, then it's your responsibility to help them. And this isn't always easy. I know it can be hard to raise a kid and even harder to raise a young entrepreneur. But if you don't step up and do what you're here to do, then they can't do what they're here to do.

Have Courage

The world doesn't normally support being weird or different or unique, and it certainly doesn't support non-traditional parenting. I know that my parents had to have courage to do things differently. Our way is to make decisions together. I get to have a say. I am able to tell them what I want. Most parents think that they're supposed to have all the answers or that they're supposed to know exactly what their child wants. That puts a lot of pressure on parents, and it makes kids feel powerless or like they don't know who they are.

An easy way to start having more courage in parenting is to allow your children to have more of a say. For instance, at restaurants, allow them to order for themselves. I see a lot of parents ordering for their kids even if their kids are ten years old or older. When I see that, I wonder why those kids can't order for themselves. Maybe they're shy or don't feel very confident in what they want.

It's a powerful thing for children to be able to speak for themselves. What my parents do is if a server asks them what I want to eat or drink, they just look at me and don't say anything. Then I get to answer for myself. Sometimes the server feels awkward, but my parents have the courage to let me be me. They let me represent myself.

Adults also like to ask parents how old their children are, even if the kids are standing right there. Have the courage to allow your children to speak for themselves.

If your children are interested in an event or a hobby that kids aren't usually involved with, have the courage to find a way to include them or allow them to participate. At least have the courage to think about it and find a new way of doing things. If you find something you think your children might like, talk with them before making decisions for them. And encourage them to be courageous too. That way they'll know they have power too.

If your kids want to do something new and it scares you a little—like zip lining, scuba diving, or parkour, for example—have the courage to let them try it or, at least, look into it. It might scare you, but it may be a clue about their purpose or how they want to live their life.

If you know your kid is here to make a difference, it's important that you have the courage to parent them differently. If you choose to parent in the same way everyone else does, then your child will be the same as everyone else.

Connect With Your Kids

The easiest way to know what your kids want and how to help them is to ask them. Communication is key. If you just assume what your kids want or need, they may feel like they're powerless or like they don't have a say in things. They will feel like you, their parents, completely control their lives. It creates a separation. Kids may start to believe that they can't do simple life skills. It limits problem solving, decision making, and critical thinking. Most people think that young kids aren't capable of knowing what they want or knowing how to do things. But they are.

If your kids are interested in business, then they need to know how to communicate. If you think and act for them then they won't get to practice communication. If you speak to them differently than you would to adults, then they might feel like they're being left out or that you don't think they can understand what you're saying. Even when I was little, my parents talked to me as if I were an equal. Even now, I'm treated like an equal, and I know that I have a say in things.

Another big benefit to connecting with your kids is they will come to you when they want to talk, when they have ideas, or when they need help. Kids want to know that their parents will listen to them and that they support them. And the best part about it is you don't have to have all the answers. Your kids know things too.

Love Yourself

As I mentioned before, it's hard to raise a child and even harder to raise a young entrepreneur. You made a decision to parent your kids differently. You will mess up.

Your kids are going to mess up, too. But that's ok. We're talking about doing things that haven't been done before. There are no rules, no instruction book, and no one can tell you exactly how to raise your child. That's between you and your kid. But there's a secret. If you remember this one thing, it makes a huge difference:

Love Yourself

When you love yourself, first off, you get to show your kids how to love themselves. This is important. Kids need examples in order to learn things. Loving yourself is the best thing you can teach your kids. Secondly, when your kids love themselves, they'll teach others how to do the same.

Be okay messing up. Apologize at the right time, and teach your kids how to do the same. Parenting a young entrepreneur is a journey, and we're all trying to figure it out.

Ask for Help

As you raise a young entrepreneur, there are going to be moments when you don't know what to do or you don't know how to help them. It's okay to ask for help.

But there's a catch. Make sure you ask people who know what they're talking about. Don't ask parenting advice about how to raise a young entrepreneur from someone who hasn't done it. Don't look for encouragement from people who don't have the courage to do things differently.

My parents are both former counterintelligence agents. They founded a firm that vets businesses, coaches, consultants, etc. They make sure that the people you're going to work with are who they say they are and can do what they say they can do. I've learned a lot from listening to their classes and paying attention to what they have to say.

Before you follow someone or hire them to help you with your young entrepreneur, make sure you ask some questions first. Make sure they're a good fit.

Working With Me

One of the questions I get asked a lot is, "How can you help parents raise a young entrepreneur when you've never raised one?" Parents come to me when they want help connecting with their child, being more playful, creating a business that's fun, and, if they're thinking about having kids or are pregnant, raising them differently.

I work with parents to help them understand the kid side of things and remind them what it was like to be a kid. Most people have never experienced their parents truly understanding and supporting them the way I have. I can help with that. I can help parents break that cycle.

One Last Thought

> *For kids, anything is possible when we have the support of our parents and other adults.*

Did you know that there are kids in this world who know who they are? They know they're here to be leaders, they know they're here to make a difference, and they know they're here to change the world—not when we become adults, but now, as kids.

But we can't do that without your support. We need the support of our parents and communities to do what we came here to do.

So here are some final tips:

1. If you're a parent, talk with your kids, include them in decisions, and connect with them each day.

2. If you run events or know someone who does, find a way to include kids. I'm always happy to speak at events and help people understand that kids are capable of business.

3. If you're a business owner, sponsor young entrepreneur ideas. Many kids out there could use support, and there are a lot of ways communities can get involved with what I do.

4. When you see kids, remember to treat them as equals. You'll be surprised what we're capable of.

5. Above all else . . . love yourself. It's contagious.

Thank you for having the courage to read a book written by a nine-year-old. And thank you for helping change the world.

Love, Neva

Next Steps

Thank you for reading my book. If you would like to have me come speak at your event, you can send a booking request to Neva@NevaLeeRecla.com.

And if you're like Joe Polish and JP Sears and would like an Oracle Card Reading, you can book a time with me at NevaLeeRecla.com.

About the Author

Neva Lee Recla is an entrepreneur, author, speaker, and inspiration. She's on a mission to inspire one million kids to do business and encourage adults to support them. She believes: *Even if kids don't want to do business, if they know they can, they'll believe they can do anything!*

At the age of two, Neva asked for her first business cards and never looked back. From her veteran philanthropy, *Spreading Light, Love, and Pixie Dust*™, to hosting the *Super Power Kids*™ podcast, she delights and impacts the world, one connection at a time.

Her motto is: We all have super powers and we can change the world!

Neva's Sponsors

Discover Your Manifesting Super Powers!

You are the hero you've been looking for. Everything you need to live an abundant, happy life is within you, now. You can do this! I'll show you how.

Author, Master Coach & Certified Hypnotherapist

kat@katwellsinternational.com

830-331-9461

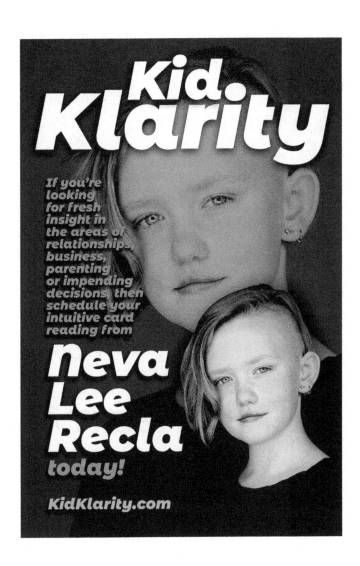

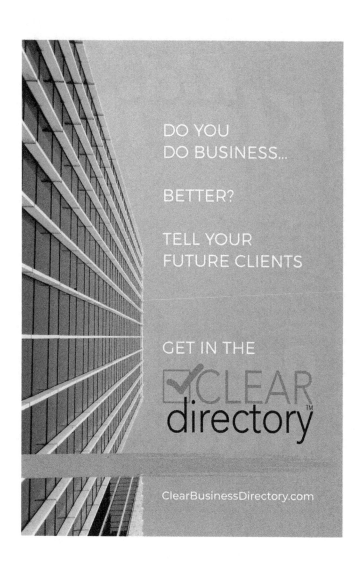

Today's the Day. Be There.

Chateau 20 is proud to support young entrepreneurs
like Neva Lee.

We're committed to supporting the next generation—
because the future depends on it.

Empowering connections that drive results ~ chateau20.com

Claire's Place Foundation, Inc.
Supporting Children with Cystic Fibrosis

TAG 4 Change Movement

Creating a New Equation for World Humanity
Homes, schools, and corporations become places where
relationships are so meaningful, everyone treats each
other with civility.

TAG 4 Change Ambassador Training Available

TAG4Change.com

Marty@TAG4Change.com

321-848-4997